STUDE
TOASTED SANDWICH
RECIPE BOOK

STUDENTS' TOASTED SANDWICH RECIPE BOOK

GILL McCORMICK

foulsham
LONDON • NEW YORK • TORONTO • SYDNEY

foulsham

The Publishing House, Bennetts Close
Cippenham, Berkshire, SL1 5AP, England

ISBN 0-572-03126-2

A CIP record for this book is available from the British Library

Previously published as *Tasty Toasties*

Printed in Great Britain by Cox & Wyman Ltd, Reading, Berkshire

So you have finally left home and are about to embark on a new phase in your life which will no doubt involve making lots of new friends, partying, drinking, sleeping in, possibly some work and, of course, cooking!

Yes, the dreaded 'C' word. If you are not predisposed to kitchen wizardry and you believe that cooking simply involves opening a can and toasting bread, this is the book for you! A sandwich toaster will probably save you precious time and money, particularly at 3am when you are slightly the worse for wear and tempted to dial for a kebab or pizza! No longer will this be necessary, because with the aid of this book, you will be able to rustle up a delicious, savoury snack in minutes!

Read through this book and be enlightened at the potential your humble sandwich toaster has. Not only can it make cheese toasties, but also mushroom omelettes, tuna and sweetcorn munchies, banana mallow desserts and tangy lemon cheesecakes!

All sandwich toasters work in a similar way and to obtain the best results you should follow the manufacturer's instructions, but I have outlined some instructions to help get you started.

Before you use a brand-new toaster for the first time, you must wipe the surface of the plates with a damp cloth and then smear them with a little butter, margarine or vegetable oil. To avoid smoke, do this before you heat the plates. Once you have turned the toaster on, you must allow it to preheat, which can be anything from 4–8 minutes, depending on the make of your toaster. Use this time to prepare your filling, pastry or dough, depending on what you fancy eating. Remember that unlike conventional sandwiches, the bread is usually buttered on the outside and the filling placed between the unbuttered sides. That way you get a lovely golden colour and a crispy texture – and bread that doesn't stick to the plates! Either place the filled sandwich on to the heated plates or make the sandwich up on the plates themselves. This is usually best if you are using pastry or a runny filling.

The amount of filling you use will depend on the thickness of the bread, pastry or dough and the depth of the toasting plates. In this book, I have used medium sliced bread and when using doughs have rolled them out thinly so that they become crisp when toasted. Don't be tempted to overfill your sandwiches because all that will happen is that they will leak when you press the lid down, causing a mess **you** will have to clean up – unless, of course, you believe that your housemates are 'pseudo-mums', willing and prepared to clean up after you without complaint!

Once you have positioned your sandwich, lower the lid to seal the toasty. Some sandwich toasters have a clip that helps to seal your toasty, but don't clip the plates together if you are cooking pastries and doughs as you need to allow them room to rise. Toasting time is really a matter of personal preference, but generally about 2-3 minutes is enough. I have quoted times with the recipes as some breads and linings can take longer than others. Depending on your model, you may notice a light on your toaster flashing on and off while you are cooking. This is not a sign that your toaster is about to short-circuit, merely an indication that the thermostat is working to keep the toaster at the right temperature.

Once your sandwich has been toasted, remove it with a nylon or wooden spatula. Try to avoid using sharp objects such as knives, even they are the only clean utensil to hand in the kitchen, as these will damage the non-stick surface. You may need to separate the sandwich halves by hand, but take care as the filling will be hot. Equally, try not to stuff it straight into your mouth as you will probably end up with a burnt tongue! If you are cooking a batch, leave the toaster on between sandwiches, but close the lid to preserve the heat.

Keeping it clean

Once you have finished making your toasties, remember to switch the toaster off, unplug it and allow it to cool with the lid raised. Once cooled, but still warm, you will be able to wipe the plates with a kitchen towel or soft cloth to remove any excess fat. If your toaster has removable plates, wait until they are cold before removing them and washing them in hot water with a gentle detergent. Don't be tempted to use abrasive scouring pads or steel wool to clean stubborn stains as these will damage the non-stick finish. Use a nylon brush that has been dipped in a hot detergent solution instead. Another trick is to pour a little cooking oil over any residual filling on the plates and wait 5 minutes until the food has softened and is easily wiped off.

Needless to say, never immerse the toaster in water. If the outside looks a little dirty, wipe it with a barely damp cloth which has been squeezed out in warm soapy water. That way, your toaster has a chance of surviving your student kitchen without conking out months before its guarantee expires!

Tips for scrummy toasties

Breads
If you are able to think ahead and are feeling really keen, try to buy bread that when sliced will cover the toasting plate properly so you don't either end up with too small and measly a sarnie or have to deal with 'overhang' that results in a soggy section of untoasted bread that will blight your masterpiece.

Be a bit adventurous with your bread. White is fine but there is a whole world of breads out there waiting to be tried, such as wholemeal, wholegrain, rye or wheatgerm. Not only will these make your toasties even more interesting, but they are full of fibre, which will help stop you feeling sluggish. There is no need to remove the crusts from your slices. In fact, leaving them on helps to form a good seal around a toasty – preventing leaks and stopping your worktop getting more of the filling than you!

Pastries and doughs
Not many people realise this but you can also cook shortcrust, puff and choux pastry, as well as doughs, quite successfully in sandwich toasters. It's not worth making your own as you can buy them chilled or frozen in any supermarket. See pages 87-90 for more information on how to make pastries and doughs.

Butter and coatings

For the sake of simplicity, I have stated 'buttered bread' in the recipes, but bacon fat, vegetable oil and different margarines can be used on breads or linings before they are toasted. Don't over-do it though because you will end up with very greasy, soggy sandwiches. One thing you can do to add interest and flavour to your toasties is to use flavoured butters, which you can then spread on the outer side of your sandwiches. See pages 91-94 for details on how to make your own flavoured butters.

If you are strapped for time but fancy coating your sandwich with something, try dipping the bread into a beaten egg. It is advisable to oil the plates well if you do this and to allow an extra minute or two for the coating to cook properly.

For those of you with a sweet tooth, sprinkling sugar onto the buttered side of the bread creates a naughty but nice coating and works especially well with sweet fillings. Try mixing butter and brown sugar together before coating your bread. It creates a delicious caramel flavour and goes down very well when the toasty is served with ice-cream!

Minis and rolls

You can also make mini toasties, pies or pizzas if your toaster is a model with plates that divide and cut sandwiches. Simply prepare your sandwich, pie or pizza and toast in the usual way, but turn it half-way through toasting to divide each half into two. Bear in mind that you may need slightly less filling than usual when making minis.

If you fancy creating something a bit different, try making a rolled sandwich. Trim the crusts from really fresh, soft slices of bread and then slightly flatten each slice with a rolling pin (or clean bottle). Butter one side of bread, and spread your chosen filling over the unbuttered side. Roll up like a Swiss roll with the buttered side out and carefully place each roll on to the pre-heated plates. If your toasted has sectioned plates, place the rolls diagonally so that the join of the roll rests against the cutter. If your model has dished plates without a cutter, place one roll, join side down, on to each plate. Lower the lid, but don't press down, and toast until golden brown. Once toasted, they can be cut into smaller rolls and served with a dip.

Leftovers
Being a novice cook, you will no doubt buy or make too much of a good thing and be left with food that you don't quite know what to do with. Don't give the rubbish bin the opportunity to put on weight – plug in your sandwich toaster instead! Try binding leftovers with a little sauce, cream cheese or mayonnaise to make instant appetising and nutritious fillings. Remember that canned foods can be teamed with leftovers to make more substantial fillings. Try to be a little imaginative, but if you are struggling for inspiration, recipes in this book that call for canned ingredients can be substituted with leftovers. If you are really in dire straits then make use of that student saviour, baked beans, which you can cook with sausages or chopped meats to make delicious and cheap fillings. Bacon slices can also be easily cooked between the toaster plates and the bacon fat used to flavour the bread. If you are a veggie, cooked potatoes or vegetables can be mashed together and mixed with herbs and a little beaten egg to create cheap and tasty vegetable cakes. Simply shape and cook the mixture between the plates without clipping the handles together. It doesn't have to be complicated to be tasty and economical!

And last but by no means least ...
Always pre-cook meat, fish and poultry thoroughly before using it as a filling in a sandwich. Your toaster can do many things but it can't cook these as thoroughly as other appliances. You don't want your conscience clouded by the thought you poisoned you and your friends! Remember to drain away any excess juice if you choose to use a canned filling to prevent your sandwiches becoming runny and a tad unappetising!

NOTES ON THE RECIPES

- Standard spoon measurements are used in all recipes:
    - 1 tablespoon (tbsp)　　=　　one 15 ml spoon
    - 1 teaspoon (tsp)　　=　　one 5 ml spoon

- All spoon measures are level unless otherwise indicated.

- Follow one set of measures only. Exact can and packet sizes have been quoted when used in a recipe.

- In this book, a sandwich comprises of two slices of bread, toasted on one plate, serving one person. Where the toaster plate divides or cuts the bread in two, this is still assumed to be one serving. These recipes were tested on dual-plated appliances. If you have a four-plated toaster, you will have to adapt the recipes accordingly.

- Occasionally you will need to flatten slices of bread. If you don't have a rolling pin, a clean bottle is just as effective.

DAIRY FILLINGS

Cheese and eggs lend themselves extremely well to the student sandwich toaster, producing tasty, cheap and nutritious fillings. Try experimenting with different types of cheeses and mixing these and hard-boiled (hard-cooked) eggs with your favourite chutneys, relishes and salad dressings.

All the sandwiches in this chapter can be served at breakfast time; as a snack at lunch time with a bowl of soup; or for early evening dinners.

BREAKFAST SPECIAL

Serves 2

15 ml/1 tbsp oil
2 rashers (slices) of smoked bacon, rinded and chopped
2 large mushrooms, finely chopped
5 ml/1 tsp butter
2 eggs, beaten
30 ml/2 tbsp milk
Salt and pepper
4 slices of bread, buttered on one side
To serve:
Sliced tomatoes

1. Heat the oil in a non-stick pan and fry (sauté) the bacon and mushrooms. Drain and place in a bowl.

2. Melt the butter in a non-stick pan.

3. Beat together the eggs, milk and salt and pepper to taste. Pour into the pan and cook slowly until the mixture is thick but still creamy.

4. Mix in the bacon and mushrooms.

5. Lay two slices of bread, buttered-side down, on to the preheated plates. Spread evenly with the egg mixture and cover with the remaining slices of bread, buttered-side up.

6. Lower the lid and toast for about 2–3 minutes until the bread is golden brown.

7. Serve with sliced tomatoes.

SALAMI SAVOURY

Serves 2

10 ml/2 tsp butter
3 eggs, lightly beaten
30 ml/2 tbsp milk
Salt and pepper
50 g/2 oz salami, cut into thin strips and chopped
4 slices of bread, buttered on one side

1. Melt the butter in a non-stick pan.

2. Mix together the eggs and milk and season with salt and pepper. Pour into the pan and cook slowly over a low heat, stirring continuously, until the mixture is thick but still creamy.

3. Add the salami and mix well.

4. Lay two slices of bread, buttered-side down, on to the preheated plates. Spread evenly with the egg mixture and cover with the remaining slices of bread, buttered-side up.

5. Lower the lid and toast for about 2–3 minutes until the bread is golden brown.

MUSHROOM OMELETTES

Serves 2

---

200 g/7 oz can of sliced mushrooms, well drained

---

2 eggs, beaten

Salt and pepper

---

4 slices of bread, spread on one side with Herb Butter (see page 92)

---

1. Mix the mushrooms and eggs together in a bowl and season well with salt and pepper.

2. Lay two slices of bread, buttered-side down, on to the preheated plates. Spread spoonfuls of the mixture slowly over the bread, allowing it to soak in. Top with the remaining slices of bread, buttered-side up.

3. Lower the lid and toast for about 2–3 minutes until the bread is golden brown.

4. Serve at breakfast time or with additional vegetables for a snack or supper.

DID YOU KNOW?

It is not true that brown eggs are better than white, nor does the colour of the yolk reveal anything about its food value or freshness.

CURRIED EGG ROLLS

Makes 8

3 hard-boiled (hard-cooked) eggs, chopped
15 ml/1 tbsp curry mayonnaise
Salt and pepper
8 slices of bread
Curry Butter (see page 92), for spreading

1. **Mix together the eggs and mayonnaise and season with salt and pepper.**

2. **Trim the crusts from the bread and flatten each slice with a rolling pin.**

3. **Spread one side lightly with the curry butter and the other with the egg filling, dividing it equally over the bread slices.**

4. **Roll up each slice of bread, buttered-side out, and place on to the preheated plates.**

5. **Lower the lid and toast for 2–3 minutes. Repeat with the remaining rolls.**

EGG AND HAM PIES

Serves 4

3 hard-boiled (hard-cooked) eggs, finely chopped
10 ml/2 tsp mayonnaise
100 g/4 oz sliced ham, chopped
2 spring onions (scallions), chopped
5 ml/1 tsp French (Dijon) mustard
Salt and pepper
350 g/12 oz frozen puff pastry, thawed
Melted butter or oil

1. Combine all the ingredients in a bowl, except the pastry and the butter, and mix well. Season to taste.

2. Divide the pastry in half and roll out each piece to approximately 25 cm/10 in square. Cut each piece into four smaller squares.

3. Brush one side of each piece with melted butter or oil and lay two, oiled-side down, on to the preheated plates. Quickly fill with some of the egg mixture, spreading it out evenly, and cover each with a pastry square, oiled-side up.

4. Lower the lid without clipping the handles together and cook for about 3–4 minutes or until the pastry is golden brown and crisp. Remove from the toaster and repeat with the remaining ingredients.

CREAMY DIPPED PARCELS

Serves 4

Oil, for brushing
100 g/4 oz full-fat soft (cream) cheese
15 ml/1 tbsp cream of onion soup mix (dried from packet)
30 ml/2 tbsp milk
200 g/7 oz canned sweetcorn (corn), drained
A dash of Worcestershire sauce
Salt and pepper
2 eggs, lightly beaten
8 slices of bread

1. Brush the non-stick plates with a little oil.

2. Mix together the cheese and onion soup mix and blend in the milk. Leave to stand for about 10–15 minutes.

3. Stir in the sweetcorn and Worcestershire sauce and season with salt and pepper.

4. Pour the beaten eggs into a large, shallow dish and season well.

5. Spread the filling equally over four slices of bread and top with the remaining slices.

6. Dip the sandwiches into the beaten egg, coating both sides. Lay two on to the preheated plates, lower the lid and cook for about 3 minutes.

7. Repeat with the remaining two. Serve immediately.

SLIMMERS' TREAT

Serves 4

150 g/5 oz cottage cheese with onion and peppers
3 lightly-boiled (soft-cooked) eggs, finely chopped
2 celery sticks, chopped
Salt and pepper
8 slices of bread, buttered on one side with low-fat spread
To serve:
Crisp green salad

1. **Mix together the cottage cheese, eggs and celery. Season with salt and pepper.**

2. **Lay two slices of bread, buttered-side down, on to the preheated plates and spread with some of the egg filling over the slices.**

3. **Cover with slices of bread, buttered-side up.**

4. **Lower the lid and toast for about 2–3 minutes.**

5. **Repeat with the remaining ingredients and serve with a crisp green salad.**

TOASTING TIP

If you are health conscious, you can leave the outside of the bread unbuttered. After toasting a number of sandwiches in this way, however, the plates may need to be re-oiled to prevent the bread or other lining sticking during toasting.

POPEYE TOASTIES

Serves 4

225 g/8 oz frozen, chopped spinach, thawed
3 hard-boiled (hard-cooked) eggs, finely chopped
200 g/7 oz can of sliced mushrooms, well-drained
5–10 ml/1–2 tsp French (Dijon) mustard
Salt and pepper
350 g/12 oz frozen puff or shortcrust pastry, thawed
Melted butter, for brushing

1. Squeeze out as much liquid as possible from the spinach. Place in a bowl and mix in the eggs, mushrooms and mustard. Season with plenty of salt and pepper.

2. Divide the pastry in half and roll each piece to approximately 25 cm/10 in square. Cut each into four smaller squares.

3. Brush one side with melted butter and lay two, buttered-side down, on to the preheated plates.

4. Quickly fill with some of the egg and spinach mixture and cover each with a pastry square, buttered-side up.

5. Lower the lid without clipping the handles together and cook for about 3 minutes or until the pastry is golden brown and crisp.

6. Remove from the toaster and then repeat with the remaining ingredients.

CREAMY ASPARAGUS DELIGHTS

Serves 4

350 g/12 oz can of asparagus cuts and tips, well drained
3 hard-boiled (hard-cooked) eggs, chopped
15 ml/1 tbsp garlic mayonnaise
Salt and pepper
8 slices of bread, buttered on one side

1. **Mix together the asparagus, eggs and mayonnaise. Season with salt and pepper.**

2. **Lay two slices of bread, buttered-side down, on to the preheated plates. Spoon over some of the egg mixture and cover with slices of bread, buttered-side up.**

3. **Lower the lid and toast for 2 minutes. Repeat with the remaining ingredients.**

4. **If your toaster has sectioned plates, then half way through toasting raise the lid and arrange the toasties so that they lie across the cutting bar to make minis.**

CHEESY CHOUX BUNS
Makes about 10

1 quantity Basic Choux Pastry (see page 88)
100 g/4 oz full-fat soft (cream) cheese
100 g/4 oz blue cheese, finely grated
15 ml/1 tbsp freshly chopped chives
60 ml/4 tbsp soured cream and chive dressing
To serve:
Lettuce and watercress

1. Place 15 ml/1 tbsp of the choux pastry mixture on each of the oiled, preheated plates. Lower the lid, without clipping the handles together, and cook for about 8–10 minutes until the pastry feels really crisp.

2. Blend together the cheeses until soft and creamy, then add the chives and dressing. Mix until smooth.

3. Remove the choux buns from the toaster, make a slit in the side of each bun and cool on a wire rack.

4. Halve the choux buns and spoon in the filling.

5. Repeat with the remaining ingredients.

DID YOU KNOW?
Blue cheese varieties include Stilton, Roquefort, Gorgonzola and Dolcelatte (a mild version of Gorgonzola). Whether soft or firm, all should have blue veins that contrast sharply and cleanly with the body of the cheese. Avoid cheeses with dark brown blotches in the body colour or in which the veins do not evenly spread throughout the cheese.

QUICK PIZZA TOASTIES

Serves 2

1 quantity Basic Scone Dough (see page 90)
15 ml/1 tbsp oil
½ small onion, chopped
50 g/2 oz mushrooms, thinly sliced
4–5 slices of garlic sausage, chopped
15 ml/1 tbsp tomato purée (paste)
1.5 ml/¼ tsp mixed dried herbs
Salt and pepper
Melted butter, for brushing
30 ml/2 tbsp Cheddar cheese, grated
To serve:
Green salad

1. **Make the scone dough and roll out thinly to measure 25 cm/10 in square. Cut into four and allow to rest.**

2. **Heat the oil in a pan and fry (sauté) the onion and mushrooms for 1–2 minutes. Drain and place in a bowl.**

3. **Mix in the garlic sausage, tomato purée, mixed herbs and salt and pepper to taste.**

4. **Brush one side of the pizza squares with melted butter and lay two, buttered-side down, on to the preheated plates. Quickly spread the filling over and sprinkle with the cheese. Place the remaining squares over the top, buttered-side up, and lower the lid. Do not clip the handles together.**

5. **Toast for about 3 minutes. Allow to stand for 1–2 minutes before serving with a green salad.**

CHEESE AND ONION PUFFS

Serves 4

1 onion, finely chopped
175 g/6 oz Cheddar cheese, finely grated
1 garlic clove, crushed (optional)
Salt and pepper
A good pinch of ground nutmeg
350 g/12 oz frozen puff pastry, thawed
Melted butter or oil
To serve:
Vegetables

1. Mix together the onion, cheese and garlic (if used). Season with salt, pepper and nutmeg to taste.

2. Divide the pastry in half and roll each piece to approximately 25 cm/10 in square. Cut each into four smaller squares.

3. Brush one side of the pastry with melted butter and lay two, buttered-side down, on to the preheated plates. Quickly fill with some of the cheese mixture. Cover each one with a pastry square, buttered-side up, and lower the lid, but do not clip the handles together.

4. Cook for about 3 minutes or until the pastry is golden brown and crisp. Repeat with the remaining ingredients.

5. These are delicious in a packed lunch or served with additional vegetables as part of a main meal.

See page 28 for variations to this recipe.

VARIATIONS

CHEESE AND CELERY
Omit the onion and garlic and add two sticks of finely chopped celery and 25 g/1 oz raisins. Bind together with a little mayonnaise.

CHEESE AND APPLE
Omit the garlic and reduce the cheese to 100 g/4 oz. Add one large, crisp, green apple, peeled, cored and finely grated.

TOASTING TIP
Avoid using processed cheeses as they tend to run during toasting. Grated cheese is better to use for toasties. Any leftover pieces of cheese in the fridge can be grated and mixed with mayonnaise or dressings to make creamy fillings. Different types of cheeses can be mixed together to make really tasty sandwiches.

MEAT FILLINGS

The fillings in this section include beef, pork, ham and lamb. The different meats have been teamed up with complementary ingredients from the storecupboard and fridge, to make substantial toasties for snacks and main meals.

Always use ready-cooked meat in the fillings, as the toasting time is so quick. Meat that is canned, freshly cooked or leftover from dinner the night before can be used to make really tasty and nourishing toasties.

STEAK AND KIDNEY PIES

Serves 4

400 g/14 oz can of steak and kidney pie filling
200 g/7 oz can of sliced mushrooms, well drained
5 ml/1 tsp French (Dijon) mustard (optional)
350 g/12 oz frozen puff pastry, thawed
Melted butter, for brushing

1. Place the pie filling in a small pan and add the mushrooms. Heat through gently and stir in the mustard. Drain and reserve the gravy.

2. Divide the pastry into half and roll out each piece to approximately 25 cm/10 in square. Cut each piece into four smaller squares. Brush one side of each piece with melted butter and lay two, buttered-side down, on to the preheated plates.

3. Using a draining spoon, quickly fill with some of the pie filling, spreading it out evenly, and cover each with a pastry square, buttered-side up. Lower the lid without clipping the handles together and cook for about 3–4 minutes, or until the pastry is golden brown and crisp.

4. Remove from the toaster and repeat with the remaining ingredients.

5. Serve the pies with a little of the warmed, reserved gravy poured over the top.

See page 31 for variations to this recipe.

VARIATIONS

STEAK AND VEGETABLE PIES
Use a small can of steak pie filling and mix with any leftover or canned vegetables.

CORNED BEEF AND POTATO PIES
Mix together a 225 g/8 oz can of corned beef and 100 g/ 4 oz cooked, diced potatoes. Season to taste and bind the mixture together with 30 ml/2 tbsp mayonnaise. Use as a filling between pastry or bread.

BEEFBURGER TOASTIES

Serves 4

---

4 beefburgers (thawed if frozen)

---

8 slices of bread, buttered on one side

Tomato ketchup (catsup) or French (Dijon) mustard, for spreading

---

1 small onion, thinly sliced into rings

---

1. Using a gentle heat, grill (broil) the beefburgers lightly on both sides until cooked through.

2. Spread the unbuttered sides of four slices of bread with either ketchup or mustard and lay two, buttered-side down, on to the preheated plates.

3. Top each with a beefburger and a few onion rings. Cover with the remaining bread, buttered-side up, lower the lid and toast for 2–3 minutes.

4. Repeat with the remaining ingredients.

NOTE

If your toaster has sectionalised plates with a divider, cut the burger in half after grilling and position it on the bread so that each half lies either side of the divider.

VARIATIONS

Top the burger with mayonnaise and tomato slices instead of onion rings, or use any burger relish of your choice.

BEEF AND CHEESE SAVOURY

Serves 2

200 g/7 oz can of minced (ground) beef with onions
5 ml/1 tsp tomato purée (paste)
2 large tomatoes, skinned and chopped
Salt and pepper
4 slices of bread, buttered on one side
50 g/2 oz Cheddar cheese, grated

1. Gently warm the minced beef in a pan and add the tomato purée and tomatoes. Mix well and season with salt and pepper to taste.

2. Lay two slices of bread, buttered-side down, on to the preheated plates. Spoon on the drained beef and tomato mixture and sprinkle with grated cheese. Cover with the remaining slices of bread, buttered-side up.

3. Lower the lid and toast for about 2–3 minutes until the bread is golden brown.

4. Serve at once, and eat with a knife and fork as the filling is fairly runny.

VARIATIONS

These are delicious when made with shortcrust pastry and served with fresh vegetables.

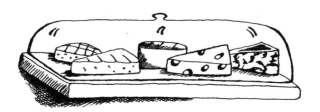

HERBY SAUSAGE ROLLS

Serves 8

8 slices of bread, crusts removed
Herb Butter (see page 92), for spreading
30 ml/2 tbsp tomato ketchup (catsup)
8 cooked skinless sausages

1. Use a rolling pin to flatten and lengthen the bread slices slightly.

2. Spread one side with herb butter and the other with tomato ketchup.

3. Roll up, with the sausage inside and the buttered side outwards. Put one roll in each section of the preheated plates or along the dished plates.

4. Toast for about 2–3 minutes and repeat with the remaining ingredients.

5. Serve as a snack with soup.

SAUSAGE BEAN FEAST

Serves 2

4 cooked skinless pork sausages, chopped
225 g/8 oz can of baked beans in tomato sauce
30 ml/2 tbsp chutney
A dash of Worcestershire sauce
Black pepper
4 slices of bread, buttered on one side

1. **Mix together all the ingredients except the bread.**

2. **Lay two slices of bread, buttered-side down, on to the preheated plates.**

3. **Spoon some of the slightly drained bean mixture over the top and cover with bread, buttered-side up.**

4. **Lower the lid and toast for about 2 minutes.**

NORFOLK PORK TOASTIES
Serves 4

15 ml/1 tbsp butter
1 small onion, finely chopped
1 large apple, peeled, cored and chopped
175 g/6 oz cooked pork, chopped
1.5 ml/¼ tsp dried sage
Salt and pepper
8 slices of bread, buttered on one side

1. Melt the butter in a pan and fry (sauté) the onion and apple until soft.

2. Fold in the pork and sage and season well with salt and pepper.

3. Lay two slices of bread, buttered-side down, on to the preheated plates. Spoon some of the pork mixture over each plate and cover with slices of bread, buttered side up. Lower the lid and toast for 2–3 minutes.

4. Repeat with the remaining ingredients. Serve hot.

VARIATIONS
A little ready-made stuffing can be added to the pork mixture to bind it together.

DID YOU KNOW?
The colour of meat is no guide to quality, as it can vary quite considerably from bright red to dark brown. When meat is cut it develops a brownish-red colour when exposed to air. Try to buy meat from a good supermarket or butcher if there is one local to you.

HAM AND PINEAPPLE CRUNCH

Serves 4

100 g/4 oz boiled ham, chopped
50 g/2 oz Cheddar cheese, grated
1.5 ml/¼ tsp prepared mustard
15 ml/1 tbsp coleslaw
2 pineapple slices, finely chopped
Salt and pepper
8 slices of bread, buttered on one side

1. **Mix together all the ingredients except the bread. Season with salt and pepper.**

2. **Lay two slices of bread, buttered-side down, on to the preheated plates.**

3. **Spoon some of the ham mixture over the bread and top with two slices of bread, buttered-side up.**

4. **Lower the lid and toast for 2–3 minutes until heated through.**

5. **Repeat with the remaining ingredients.**

BACON AND MUSHROOM CHOUX BUNS

Makes about 10

1 quantity Basic Choux Pastry (see page 88)
175 g/6 oz lean bacon, finely chopped
175 g/6 oz mushrooms, finely sliced
75–90 ml/5–6 tbsp thick garlic mayonnaise

1. Place 15 ml/1 tbsp of the choux pastry mixture on each of the oiled preheated plates. Lower the lid and cook for about 8–10 minutes or until the pastry feels really crisp.

2. Meanwhile, fry (sauté) the bacon and mushrooms in a non-stick pan. Drain well and allow to cool.

3. Add sufficient mayonnaise to form a thick sauce, taking care not to let the mixture get too runny.

4. Remove the choux buns from the toaster and repeat with the remaining ingredients. Make a slit in the side of each bun and cool on a wire rack.

5. Halve the buns and spoon in the filling. Serve hot.

SPICY LAMB PIES

Serves 4

15 ml/1 tbsp oil
1 small onion, finely chopped
1 garlic clove, crushed
50 g/2 oz mushrooms, finely sliced
225 g/8 oz can of tomatoes, well drained
100 g/4 oz cooked lamb, chopped
2.5 ml/½ tsp Worcestershire sauce
Salt and pepper
350 g/12 oz frozen puff pastry, thawed
Melted butter, for brushing

1. Heat the oil in a pan and fry (sauté) the onion, garlic and mushrooms until soft.

2. Add the canned tomatoes, lamb and Worcestershire sauce. Season with salt and pepper.

3. Divide the pastry in half and roll out each piece to about 25 cm/10 in square. Cut each into four smaller squares.

4. Brush one side of each piece with melted butter and lay two, buttered-side down, on to the preheated plates.

5. Quickly fill with some of the lamb mixture, spreading it out evenly, and cover with a pastry square, buttered-side up. Lower the lid, without clipping the handles together, and cook for about 3–4 minutes until golden brown and crisp.

6. Remove from the toaster and repeat with the remaining ingredients.

CURRIED MEAT TOASTIES

Serves 2

175 g/6 oz lightly cooked or leftover meat, finely chopped
15 ml/1 tbsp garlic mayonnaise
15 ml/1 tbsp tomato ketchup (catsup)
A squeeze of lemon juice
10 ml/2 tsp grated onion
5 ml/1 tsp curry powder
3 drops of Tabasco sauce
4 slices of bread, buttered on one side
To serve:
Crisp green salad

1. Combine all the ingredients except the bread in a bowl and mix well.

2. Lay two slices of bread, buttered-side down, on to the preheated plates and spoon the meat mixture over the top. Cover with the remaining slices of bread, buttered-side up.

3. Lower the lid and toast for about 2 minutes and serve with a crisp green salad.

POULTRY FILLINGS

Chicken and turkey combine well with all manner of flavourings. Try mixing leftover chicken pieces with your favourite herbs, spices, mayonnaises and sauces to make really delicious fillings.

To make tasty fillings always use ready-cooked poultry, either leftover from a roast (if you've been adventurous enough to try to do one) or from cooked chicken portions. Cans of chicken in sauces are also handy to have in the storecupboard in case you get peckish.

TURKEY PARCELS

Serves 4

15 ml/1 tbsp butter
1 leek, trimmed to about 15 cm/6 in, thinly sliced
175 g/6 oz cooked turkey pieces, chopped
half a 200 g/7 oz can of sweetcorn (corn), drained
125 g/4½ oz canned chicken 'toast topper'
Salt and pepper
350 g/12 oz frozen shortcrust pastry, thawed
Melted butter, for brushing

1. **Melt the butter in a pan and fry (sauté) the leek until soft. Add the turkey and sweetcorn. Mix in the can of 'toast topper' and season with salt and pepper.**

2. **Divide the pastry in half and roll out each piece to approximately 25 cm/10 in square. Cut each into four smaller squares.**

3. **Brush one side of each piece with melted butter and lay two, buttered-side down, on the preheated plates.**

4. **Quickly fill with some of turkey mixture, spreading it out evenly and cover each with a pastry square, buttered-side up.**

5. **Lower the lid, but do not clip the handles together, and cook for about 3 minutes or until the pastry is golden brown and crisp.**

6. **Remove from the toaster and repeat with the remaining ingredients.**

CELEBRATION TURKEY

Serves 4

15 ml/1 tbsp butter or margarine
1 small onion, chopped
1 garlic clove, crushed
225 g/8 oz cooked turkey pieces, chopped
5 ml/1 tsp lemon juice
5 ml/1 tsp curry powder
5 ml/1 tsp tomato purée (paste)
10 ml/2 tsp apricot jam (conserve)
30–45 ml/2–3 tbsp mayonnaise
1 small apple, peeled, cored and chopped
Salt and pepper
8 slices of bread, buttered on one side

1. **Melt the butter in a pan and fry (sauté) the onion and garlic until soft.**

2. **Add the turkey pieces and the remaining ingredients, except the bread. Mix well and season to taste with salt and pepper.**

3. **Place two slices of bread, buttered-side down, on to the preheated plates and spoon some of the turkey mixture over the top.**

4. **Cover with slices of bread, buttered-side up. Lower the lid and toast for about 2 minutes.**

5. **Repeat with the remaining ingredients.**

CHINESE CHICKEN

Makes 4

15 ml/1 tbsp white wine
175 g/6 oz cooked chicken pieces, chopped
50 g/2 oz beansprouts or white cabbage, finely shredded
2 slices of cooked ham, chopped
25 g/1 oz almonds, chopped
1.5 g/¼ tsp ground ginger
30 ml/2 tbsp mayonnaise
A dash of soy sauce
Salt and pepper
8 slices of bread, buttered on one side

1. Pour the wine over the chicken and, if time is available, leave in the fridge for about 1 hour.

2. Mix in the beansprouts or white cabbage, ham, almonds and ground ginger. Stir in the mayonnaise and add a dash of soy sauce and salt and pepper to taste.

3. Lay two pieces of bread, buttered-side down, on to the preheated plates and spoon some of the chicken mixture over the top. Cover with slices of bread, buttered-side up.

4. Lower the lid and toast for about 2 minutes until the bread is golden brown. Repeat with the remaining ingredients.

SPANISH CHICKEN ROLLS

Serves 4

75 g/3 oz jar of chicken paste
4 stuffed green olives, thinly sliced
Salt and pepper
4 slices of bread, crusts removed
Softened butter, for spreading

1. **Mix together the chicken paste and olives and season to taste.**

2. **Using a rolling pin, roll out the slices of bread, to flatten and lengthen them slightly.**

3. **Spread one side of each slice with softened butter and spread the chicken paste mixture on the other.**

4. **Roll up, with the buttered-side outwards. Place on the preheated plates and toast for 2–3 minutes before serving hot.**

NOTE

If your toaster has sectioned plates, place one roll each side of the divider. For dished plates, place one roll on each plate.

CREAMY PEPPERED CHICKEN

Serves 4

50 g/2 oz full-fat soft (cream) cheese
30 ml/2 tbsp natural yoghurt
2.5 ml/½ tsp paprika
1.5–2.5 ml/¼–½ tsp soy sauce
175 g/6 oz cooked chicken pieces, chopped
½ red (bell) pepper, seeded and chopped
Salt and pepper
8 slices of bread, buttered on one side
To serve:
Fresh mixed salad

1. Mix together the cheese and yoghurt until smooth. Add the paprika and soy sauce.

2. Fold in the chicken and red pepper and mix well. Season to taste with salt and pepper.

3. Lay two slices of bread, buttered-side down, on to the preheated plates and spoon some of the chicken mixture over the top. Cover with bread, buttered-side up.

4. Lower the lid and toast for 2–3 minutes until the bread is golden brown.

5. Repeat with the remaining ingredients.

6. Serve with a fresh mixed salad.

BARBECUE CHICKEN TOASTIES

Serves 4

15 ml/1 tbsp oil
1 small onion, chopped
½ green (bell) pepper, seeded and chopped
5 ml/1 tsp soft brown sugar
30 ml/2 tbsp tomato ketchup (catsup)
10 ml/2 tsp Worcestershire sauce
225 g/8 oz cooked chicken pieces, chopped
Salt and pepper
8 slices of bread, buttered on one side
To serve:
Tossed green salad

1. **Heat the oil in a pan and fry (sauté) the onion and pepper until soft. Remove the pan from the heat.**

2. **Add the remaining ingredients, except the bread. Season and mix well together.**

3. **Lay two slices of bread, buttered-side down, on to the preheated plates and spoon some of the chicken mixture over the top. Cover with slices of bread, buttered-side up.**

4. **Lower the lid and toast for 2–3 minutes. Repeat with the remaining ingredients and serve with a green salad.**

CHICKEN AND PINEAPPLE PIZZA

Serves 4

1 quantity Basic Yeast Dough (see page 89)
Oil
1 small onion, finely chopped
1 garlic clove, crushed
1 small stick of celery, thinly sliced
half a 225 g/8 oz can of pineapple pieces, drained and chopped
175 g/6 oz cooked chicken pieces, chopped
Salt and pepper
Melted butter for brushing
45–60 ml/3–4 tbsp tomato purée (paste)
50 g/2 oz cheese, thinly sliced
To serve:
Salad and jacket potatoes

1. Cut the yeast dough in half and roll out each piece thinly. Cut into eight 13 cm/5 in squares.

2. Heat the oil in a pan and fry (sauté) the onion, garlic and celery until soft. Add the pineapple and chicken pieces, mix well and season to taste with salt and pepper.

3. Brush one side of the dough squares with melted butter and lay two, buttered-side down, on to the preheated plates. Quickly brush with tomato purée and place a little of the chicken mixture over the top. Top with sliced cheese and cover with dough squares, buttered-side up.

4. Lower the lid and toast for about 3 minutes until the dough is golden brown and crisp. Repeat with the remaining ingredients.

5. Serve immediately with salad and jacket potatoes.

TOASTING TIP

Mix together leftover chicken pieces with parsley and thyme stuffing to make a really tasty filling. Bind with a little gravy and place between bread or puff or shortcrust pastry.

CHICKEN AND TARRAGON CHOUX BUNS

Makes about 10

1 quantity of Basic Choux Pastry (see page 88)
15 ml/1 oz butter
1 small onion, finely chopped
25 g/1 oz plain (all-purpose) flour
300 ml/½ pt chicken stock
5 ml/1 tsp dried tarragon
225 g/8 oz cooked chicken, chopped
Salt and pepper

1. Place 15 ml/1 tbsp of the choux pastry on each side of the oiled and preheated plates.

2. Lower the lid and cook for about 8–10 minutes until the pastry feels really crisp.

3. Meanwhile make the sauce. Melt the butter in a pan and fry (sauté) the onion until soft. Add the flour and cook gently for 1 minute.

4. Gradually stir in the chicken stock and bring to the boil, stirring constantly. Add the tarragon and simmer for 2–3 minutes.

5. Allow the sauce to cool slightly, then fold in the chicken. Season to taste with salt and pepper.

6. Remove the choux buns from the toaster, make a slit in the side of each bun and cool on a wire rack.

7. Half the buns and spoon in the filling. Serve immediately.

CHICKEN TONNATO

Serves 4

75 g/3 oz canned tuna fish, drained and flaked
3 anchovy fillets, chopped
15 ml/1 tbsp capers, chopped
5 ml/1 tsp lemon juice
10 ml/2 tsp chopped parsley
2.5 ml/½ tsp Worcestershire sauce
60 ml/4 tbsp garlic mayonnaise
175 g/6 oz cooked chicken, chopped
Black pepper
8 slices of bread, buttered on one side
To serve:
Tossed green salad

1. Place the tuna fish in a bowl and mix in the anchovy fillets, capers, lemon juice and parsley.

2. Add the Worcestershire sauce and blend in the mayonnaise. Fold in the chicken and stir well. Season with black pepper.

3. Divide the chicken mixture equally over the unbuttered sides of four slices of bread, and top with the remaining slices, buttered-sides up.

4. Place two sandwiches between the preheated plates and toast for 2 minutes until the bread is golden brown.

5. Repeat with the remaining sandwiches and serve with a green salad.

NUTTY CHICKEN SNACKS

Serves 2

100 g/4 oz cooked chicken pieces, chopped

1 small carrot, finely grated

30 ml/2 tbsp crunchy peanut butter

A dash of Worcestershire sauce (optional)

4 slices of wholemeal bread, buttered lightly on one side

To serve:

Vegetable soup

1. In a bowl, mix together the chicken, carrot and peanut butter. Add a dash of Worcestershire sauce if you like.

2. Divide the mixture equally over the unbuttered-sides of two slices of bread and top with the remaining slices, buttered-side up.

3. Place the two sandwiches between the preheated plates and toast for 2–3 minutes.

4. Serve hot with vegetable soup for a really nourishing and tasty snack.

FISH FILLINGS

Fish is one of the most important sources of protein in our diet and both freshly cooked and canned fish make substantial and nourishing toasties, not to mention excellent brain food during exam time! It can be bought cheaply from the frozen food section in the supermarket. Due to the short-fibred flesh and the small amount of connective tissue, fish is easily digested and mixes well with sauces and seafood dressings to make creamy fillings. Remember to remove any bones from cooked fish before mixing it with other ingredients.

HUNGARIAN FISH TOASTIES

Serves 4

15 ml/1 tbsp butter
1 small onion, finely chopped
1 small garlic clove, crushed (optional)
225 g/8 oz cooked cod, flaked
5 ml/1 tsp paprika
30 ml/2 tbsp tomato purée (paste)
225 g/8 oz can of tomatoes, well-drained and chopped
Salt and pepper
8 slices of bread, buttered on one side
To serve:
Crisp green salad

1. **Melt the butter in a pan and fry (sauté) the onion and garlic until soft. Add the remaining ingredients except the bread. Mix well and season with salt and pepper.**

2. **Lay two slices of bread, buttered-side down, on to the preheated plates. Spoon over some of the fish mixture and cover with slices of bread, buttered-side up.**

3. **Lower the lid and toast for about 2 minutes or until the bread is golden brown. Repeat with the remaining ingredients.**

4. **These toasties are delicious served hot with a crisp green salad.**

FISH FLORENTINES

Serves 4

225 g/8 oz packet of frozen, chopped spinach, thawed
175 g/6 oz cooked white fish (e.g. cod, haddock), flaked
A squeeze of lemon juice
30 ml/2 tbsp mayonnaise
Salt and pepper
8 slices of bread, buttered on one side
Parmesan cheese, finely grated, to taste

1. Squeeze out as much water as possible from the spinach. Place in a bowl and mix in the fish, lemon juice and mayonnaise. Season with plenty of salt and pepper.

2. Lay two slices of bread, buttered-side down, on to the preheated plates and spoon over some of the fish mixture.

3. Sprinkle generously with Parmesan cheese and top with slices of bread, buttered-side up.

4. Lower the lid and toast for 2–3 minutes. Repeat with the remaining ingredients.

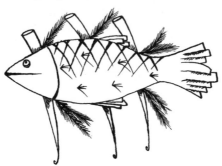

SALMON FISH CAKES

Serves 2–4

225 g/8 oz canned salmon, drained and flaked
175 g/6 oz cooked mashed potato
5 ml/1 tsp tomato purée (paste)
15 ml/1 tbsp finely chopped onion
15 ml/1 tbsp parsley, finely chopped
1 large egg, beaten
Salt and pepper
Flour
Oil, for brushing

1. Place the salmon and potato into a bowl and mix well.

2. Add the tomato purée, onion, parsley and a little beaten egg to form a stiff mixture (if using instant potato make it a little stiffer than usual). Season to taste with salt and pepper.

3. Divide the mixture into four and shape to fit the plates.

4. Roll in flour and dip in the remaining beaten egg. Place on the oiled preheated plates.

5. Lower the lid without clipping the handles together and cook for about 5 minutes until the cakes are brown on the outside.

NOTE

Lift the lid carefully after cooking to avoid breaking the fish cake. If your toaster has sectioned plates, shape the mixture to fit each side of the cutter. For dished plates, shape each cake into flat rounds and place one cake on each preheated plate.

LEMON SARDINE ROLLS

Makes about 10

100 g/4 oz canned sardines in tomato sauce
50 g/2 oz full-fat soft (cream) cheese
A squeeze of lemon juice
Black pepper
10 slices of brown bread
Lemon Butter (see page 93), for spreading

1. Mash the sardines, cheese and lemon juice together in a bowl and season to taste with black pepper.

2. Trim the crusts from the bread and flatten the slices with a rolling pin to lengthen them slightly.

3. Spread one side lightly with lemon butter and the other side with the sardine filling.

4. Roll up each slice of bread, buttered-side out, and place on the preheated plates. Lower the lid and toast for 2 minutes. Repeat with the remaining rolls.

5. These rolls are best served warm when they are deliciously crisp.

TOASTING TIP

Curried fish snacks are delicious made with any leftover white fish. Mix together a little curry sauce (either home-made or from a can) with some flaked white fish. Add a few sultanas (golden raisins) or a little grated apple and season to taste with salt and pepper. Use as a tasty filling between slices of bread.

MACKEREL SURPRISE
Serves 4

200 g/7 oz can of mackerel in brine, drained
1 small onion, finely chopped
A squeeze of lemon juice
Grated rind of ½ lemon
5 ml/1 tsp prepared English mustard
15 ml/1 tbsp finely chopped parsley
Salt and pepper
8 slices of bread, buttered on one side
To serve:
Tomato salad

1. Place the fish in a bowl and mash it with a fork.

2. Add the onion, lemon juice and rind, mustard and parsley. Mix well and season with salt and pepper.

3. Lay two slices of bread, buttered-side down, on to the preheated plates and spoon over some of the fish mixture over the top. Cover with slices of bread, buttered-side up.

4. Lower the lid and toast for about 2–3 minutes. Repeat with the remaining ingredients.

5. Serve as a snack or at dinner time with a tomato salad.

TUNA AND SWEETCORN MUNCHIES

Serves 4

200 g/7 oz canned tuna, drained and flaked

200 g/7 oz canned sweetcorn (corn), drained

30–45 ml/2–3 tbsp tartare sauce

Salt and pepper

350 g/12 oz frozen puff pastry, thawed

Melted butter for brushing

1 large tomato, thinly sliced

To serve:

Potatoes and green vegetables

1. Mix together the tuna and sweetcorn. Add tartare sauce to taste. Season with salt and pepper.

2. Divide the pastry in half and roll out each piece to approximately 25 cm/10 in square. Cut each into four smaller squares.

3. Brush one side of each piece with melted butter and lay two, buttered-side down, on to the preheated plates.

4. Quickly fill with some of the fish mixture and with slices of tomato. Cover each with a pastry square, buttered-side up.

5. Lower the lid, without clipping the handles together, and cook for about 3 minutes, or until the pastry is golden brown and crisp.

6. Repeat with the remaining ingredients.

7. Serve with potatoes and green vegetables.

CREAMY MACKEREL CHOUX BUNS

Makes about 10

1 quantity Basic Choux Pastry (see page 88)
1 smoked mackerel, skinned and boned
30 ml/2 tbsp soured cream
30 ml/2 tbsp horseradish sauce
Salt and pepper
To garnish:
Sliced tomato

1. Place 15 ml/1 tbsp of the choux pastry mixture on each of the oiled, preheated plates. Lower the lid and cook for about 8–10 minutes until the pastry feels really crisp.

2. Meanwhile, mash the mackerel in a bowl with a fork, and place into a saucepan.

3. Add the soured cream and horseradish sauce. Mix well and season with salt and pepper. Heat through very gently.

4. Remove the choux buns from the toaster, make a slit in the side of each bun and cool on a wire rack.

5. Halve the choux buns and spoon in the filling.

6. Serve at once, garnished with slices of tomato.

CURRIED KIPPER TOASTIES

Serves 4

200 g/7 oz packet of frozen, boil-in-the-bag kipper fillets
15 ml/1 tbsp butter
1 small onion, finely chopped
100 g/4 oz mushrooms, finely sliced
2.5–5 ml/½–1 tsp curry powder
A squeeze of lemon juice
Salt and pepper
8 slices of bread, buttered on one side

1. Cook the kipper fillets according to the packet instructions. Remove any skin and bones from the fillets and mash the flesh together with the juices.

2. Melt the butter in a pan and fry (sauté) the onion and mushrooms until soft. Add the kippers, curry powder and lemon juice to the pan and mix well. Season with salt and pepper.

3. Lay two slices of bread, buttered-side down, on to the preheated plates and spoon over some of the kipper mixture. Cover with slices of bread, buttered-side up. Lower the lid and toast for about 2 minutes until the bread is golden brown.

4. Repeat with the remaining ingredients.

SEAFOOD SPECIALS

Serves 4

175 g/6 oz canned crab meat, drained
250 g/9 oz canned mussels, drained
15 ml/1 tbsp finely chopped onion
A squeeze of lemon juice
45 ml/3 tbsp canned condensed lobster or crab bisque, reserving the rest
8 slices of bread, buttered on one side

1. **Mix together all the ingredients except the bread.**

2. **Place two slices of bread, buttered-side down, on to the preheated plates and spoon over some of the seafood mixture. Cover with slices of bread, buttered-side up. Lower the lid and toast for about 2 minutes.**

3. **Repeat with the remaining ingredients.**

4. **Meanwhile, make up the reserved soup according to the can instructions and serve hot with the toasties.**

TOASTING TIP

For a really delicious snack, mix together a can of drained crab meat with a little tartare sauce and lemon juice. Season to taste. Place between slices of bread or sheets of puff pastry. If your toaster has a cutter, then turn the sandwiches halfway through toasting to make minis (see page 12).

SUPPER SHRIMP PIES

Serves 4

200 g/7 oz canned prawns (shrimps) in brine, drained
75 g/3oz mature Cheddar cheese, grated
1 large hard-boiled (hard-cooked) egg, chopped
30 ml/2 tbsp seafood dressing
A dash of Worcestershire sauce
Salt and pepper
225 g/8 oz frozen shortcrust pastry, thawed
Melted butter for brushing

1. Place the prawns in a bowl and mix in the cheese, egg and seafood dressing. Add the Worcestershire sauce plus salt and pepper.

2. Roll out the pastry and cut out eight 13 cm/5 in squares. Brush one side with melted butter and lay two, buttered-side down, on to the preheated plates.

3. Quickly fill with some of the prawn mixture and cover with squares of pastry, buttered-side up.

4. Lower the lid, without clipping the handles together, and cook for about 3 minutes until the pastry is golden brown and crisp.

5. Repeat with the remaining ingredients and serve hot.

SALMON TARTARE ROLLS

Serves 4

4 slices of bread, crusts removed, buttered on one side

1 small jar of salmon paste

15 ml/1 tbsp tartare sauce or ready-made sandwich spread

1 Flatten the slices of bread with a rolling pin.

2 Spread the salmon paste over the unbuttered sides and then spread with a little tartare sauce or sandwich spread. Roll up, buttered-sides out.

3 Put one roll in each section of the preheated plates and toast for 2–3 minutes or until the bread is golden.

NOTE

You can make your own tartare sauce – just mix 10 ml/ 2 tsp salad cream with a chopped cornichon or a piece of dill pickle.

Any leftover vegetables, combined with your favourite sauces, chutneys and mayonnaises, make ideal toasties to serve with sliced meats or simply on their own as a snack. If you are vegetarian, choose recipes from this section and serve the toasties with additional protein foods such as nuts and pulses.

Vegetables are high in vitamins, minerals and fibre, so the fillings make nutritious and tasty snacks. Cooked and mashed vegetables can be used to make delicious 'cakes', which do not require any lining of bread or pastry. Try making the Carrot and Parsnip Cakes on page 66 and serve them as an accompaniment with cooked meats.

CARROT AND PARSNIP CAKES

Makes 4

175 g/6 oz cooked carrots, mashed
175 g/6 oz cooked parsnips, mashed
75 g/3 oz fresh white or brown breadcrumbs
Salt and pepper
1 egg, beaten
Oil, for brushing

1. Mix together the carrots, parsnips and breadcrumbs and season to taste with salt and pepper. Bind together with a little beaten egg to form a stiff mixture.

2. Divide into four and shape to fit the plates. Place the 'cakes' on the oiled, preheated plates.

3. Lower the lid, but do not clip the handles together, and cook for about 4 minutes until the outside is crispy.

NOTE

If your toaster has sectioned plates, place the mixture on both sides of the cutter. For dished plates, shape the mixture into flat rounds and place one on each plate. Repeat with the remaining ingredients.

DID YOU KNOW?

When buying root vegetables (such as carrots, parsnips, turnips, potatoes) they should be firm to the touch, a good colour and with skins free from blemishes. Try to choose ones of medium size as very large vegetables can be coarse and woody. At home, store the vegetables in a cool, dark place where the air can circulate round them, preferably in a vegetable rack.

NUTTY POTATO CAKES

Makes 4–5

350 g/12 oz cooked potatoes, mashed
225 g/8 oz cooked turnips, mashed
1 large egg, beaten
Salt and pepper
2.5 ml/½ tsp grated nutmeg
75–100 g/3–4 oz mixed nuts, finely chopped
Oil, for brushing

1. Mix together the potatoes and turnips. Bind the mixture together with a little beaten egg and season to taste with salt, pepper and nutmeg.

2. Divide the mixture into four or five and shape to fit the plates (see note to Carrot and Parsnip Cakes on page 66).

3. Coat the 'cakes' in the remaining beaten egg and chopped nuts. Place on the oiled, preheated plates.

4. Lower the lid, but do not clip the handles together, and cook for about 3–5 minutes or until the nuts are golden brown.

5. Remove from the toaster, together with any nuts left on the plates. Serve hot.

CURRIED VEGETABLE TOASTIES

Makes 4

15 ml/1 tbsp butter
1 small onion, finely chopped
350 g/12 oz cooked mixed vegetables (e.g. potatoes, carrots), diced
5 ml/1 tsp curry powder
15 ml/1 tbsp mango chutney
A squeeze of lemon juice
Salt and pepper
8 slices of bread, buttered on one side

1. Melt the butter in a pan and fry (sauté) the onion until soft. Add the remaining ingredients except the bread and stir well.

2. Place two slices of bread, buttered-side down, on to the preheated plates and spoon over some of the vegetable mixture. Cover with two slices of bread, buttered-side up.

3. Lower the lid and toast for about 2–3 minutes. Repeat with the remaining ingredients. Serve hot.

VARIATIONS

Use pastry instead of the bread to make curried pies.

LEEK AND TOMATO PIES

Serves 4

2 leeks, washed and trimmed to about 20 cm/8 in, thinly sliced
350 g/12 oz frozen shortcrust pastry, thawed
50 g/2 oz full-fat soft (cream) cheese, softened
15 ml/1 tbsp tomato purée (paste)
A dash of Worcestershire sauce
Salt and pepper
Melted butter, for brushing
1 large tomato, peeled and sliced

1. Lightly boil the leeks in salted water until just tender. Drain well.

2. Meanwhile, cut the pastry in half and roll out each piece to approximately 25 cm/10 in square. Cut each into four smaller squares.

3. Mix together the leeks, cheese, tomato purée, Worcestershire sauce and salt and pepper to taste.

4. Brush one side of each piece of pastry with melted butter and lay two, buttered-side down, on to the preheated plates. Quickly spoon over some of the leek mixture and top with tomato slices. Cover with pastry squares, buttered-side up.

5. Lower the lid, but do not clip the handles together, and cook for about 3 minutes or until the pastry is golden brown and crisp.

6. Repeat with the remaining ingredients. Serve hot.

SPICY MUSHROOM DEVILS

Serves 2

15 ml/1 tbsp butter
1 small onion, finely chopped
225 g/8 oz mushrooms, thinly sliced
30 ml/2 tbsp chutney
5–10 ml/1–2 tsp Worcestershire sauce
15 ml/1 tbsp chopped fresh parsley
Salt and pepper
4 slices of bread, buttered on one side

1. Melt the butter in a pan and fry (sauté) the onion and mushrooms until soft.

2. Place the slightly drained mixture in a bowl and add the chutney, Worcestershire sauce, parsley and salt and pepper to taste. Stir well.

3. Lay two slices of bread, buttered-side down, on to the preheated plates.

4. Spoon over the mushroom mixture and cover with the remaining slices of bread, buttered-side up.

5. Lower the lid and toast for about 2 minutes.

TOASTING TIP

The addition of sesame seeds sprinkled on the buttered side of the bread and pressed in, before toasting, gives a lovely flavour to the toasties. The seeds are rich in Vitamin B and their flavour is greatly improved by toasting. Remember to remove any remaining seeds from the plates afterwards.

You have slaved all day writing notes and essays or revising for an exam and want something a little indulgent to reward yourself for all your hard work. Look no further than this chapter where I will show you how to make delicious desserts and cakes such as Chocolate Profiteroles, Chocolate and Apricot Munchies and Quick Bakewell Tarts. Sound tempting? They are and I can assure you that they are simple to make in your sandwich toaster.

One word of warning: some of the fillings in the following pages can be quite runny, so I would advise you to eat them on a plate and use a knife and fork. A kitchen towel could come in quite handy as well!

PINEAPPLE AND GINGER CREAMS

Makes 2

150 ml/¼ pt thick custard (canned or home-made)
225 g/8 oz canned pineapple pieces, well-drained and chopped
1–2 lumps of stem ginger, very finely chopped
4 slices of bread, buttered on one side
Sugar, for sprinkling

1. Mix the custard, pineapple and ginger in a basin.

2. Sprinkle the buttered side of the bread with sugar and lay two slices, sugared and buttered-side down on to the preheated plates.

3. Spoon over the custard mixture and cover with the remaining slices of bread, sugared and buttered side up.

4. Lower the lid, but do not clip the handles together, and toast for about 2–3 minutes.

VARIATIONS

Use creamed rice instead of the custard and any canned or fresh fruit of your choice.

BANANA MALLOW DESSERT
Makes 2

4 slices of bread, buttered on one side
Sugar, for sprinkling
1 banana, peeled and sliced
6 marshmallows, chopped

1. Sprinkle the buttered-side of the bread with sugar and lay two slices, sugared and buttered-side down, onto the preheated plates.

2. Arrange the sliced banana over the bread and then sprinkle with the marshmallows. Cover with the remaining slices of bread, sugared and buttered-side up.

3. Lower the lid and toast for about 2 minutes.

4. Serve immediately.

NOTE
A quick way to cut the marshmallows is to use a pair of kitchen scissors.

TANGY LEMON CHEESECAKES

Makes 2

25 g/1 oz sultanas (golden raisins)
45 ml/3 tbsp lemon juice
100 g/4 oz cottage cheese
25 g/1 oz caster (superfine) sugar
Grated rind of ½ lemon
4 slices of bread, buttered on one side

1. Put the sultanas into a pan with the lemon juice, and bring slowly to the boil. Remove from the heat, drain and allow to cool.

2. Mix the cottage cheese, caster sugar and lemon rind in a bowl and add to the drained sultanas.

3. Place two slices of bread, buttered-side down, on to the preheated plates and spoon over the cottage cheese mixture. Cover with the remaining slices of bread, buttered-side up.

4. Lower the lid and toast for 2–3 minutes.

CHOCOLATE PROFITEROLES

Makes about 10

1 quantity Basic Choux Pastry (see page 88)
300 ml/½ pt double (heavy) cream, lightly whipped
225 g/8 oz icing (confectioners') sugar, sifted
15 ml/1 tbsp cocoa (unsweetened chocolate) powder
15 ml/1 tbsp rum (optional)
15–30 ml/1–2 tbsp warm water

1. Place 15 ml/1 tbsp of the choux pastry on each of the oiled, preheated plates.

2. Lower the lid and cook for about 8–10 minutes until the pastry feels really crisp.

3. Remove the choux buns from the toaster, make a slit in the side of each bun and cool on a wire rack.

4. Halve the buns and, when cold, fill with whipped cream. Pile up in a pyramid on a plate.

5. Make the chocolate glacé icing (frosting) by placing the icing sugar and cocoa in a bowl. Stir in the rum (if used) and sufficient warm water to form a thick icing. Pour over the buns, coating each one and serve immediately.

DID YOU KNOW?

Double (heavy) cream will whip more smoothly and to a greater volume if 15 ml/1 tbsp of milk is added to every 150 ml/¼ pt. A whisked egg white or a little yoghurt or soured cream can be folded into whipped double cream to lighten the texture and to make it go further.

MANDARIN SUNSETS

Makes 3

50 g/2 oz full-fat soft (cream) cheese

15 ml/1 tbsp marmalade

6 slices of bread, spread on one side with Orange Butter (see page 94)

300 g/11 oz canned mandarin orange segments, well-drained

1. Stir together the cheese and marmalade and spread the mixture over the unbuttered sides of the bread.

2. Lay two of the slices, buttered-side down, on to the preheated plates. Sprinkle over some of the orange segments and cover with slices of bread, buttered-side up.

3. Lower the lid and toast for about 2 minutes.

4. Repeat with the remaining ingredients and serve warm.

GOOSEBERRY AND GINGER TOASTIES

Makes 2

2 eggs, beaten
1.5 ml/¼ tsp ground ginger
4 slices of bread, buttered on one side
Oil
275 g/10 oz canned gooseberries, drained
Brown sugar, for sprinkling
To serve:
Whipped cream or ice-cream

1. Beat the eggs and ginger together in a flat dish.

2. Press two slices of bread, buttered-side down, into the egg mixture and lay them, buttered and egg-side down, on to the well-oiled, preheated plates.

3. Sprinkle over the gooseberries and brown sugar.

4. Dip the remaining slices of bread, buttered-side down, into the rest of the egg and lay them, buttered and egg-side up, on top.

5. Lower the lid and toast for about 3–4 minutes, or until the outside is golden brown and crisp.

6. Serve immediately with whipped cream or ice-cream.

VARIATIONS

Try flavouring the egg with ground cinnamon and fill the toasties with stewed apple.

PEAR AND CHOCOLATE ROLLS

Makes 4

4 slices of bread, crusts removed
Softened butter
Chocolate spread
200 g/7 oz canned pears, drained and mashed

1. Roll out the slices of bread with a rolling pin, to flatten and lengthen them slightly. Spread one side of each slice evenly with softened butter, and chocolate spread on the other.

2. Cover the chocolate spread with the pears and roll up with the buttered-side outwards.

3. Press the join down on to the table to seal it, and put one roll in each section of the toaster, or, for dished plates, one on each plate.

4. Lower the lid and toast for about 2–3 minutes until the rolls are brown and crisp.

VARIATION

Use a medium-soft pear, peeled, cored and mashed, or any tinned or fresh fruit of your choice.

CREAMY ALMOND COCKTAILS

Makes 2

200 g/7 oz canned fruit cocktail, well-drained

50 g/2 oz full-fat soft (cream) cheese, softened

25 g/1 oz ground almonds

1.5 ml/1/4 tsp almond essence (extract)

4 slices of bread, spread with Caramel Butter (see page 94)

To serve:

Whipped cream

1. Stir the fruit cocktail into the softened cheese and fold in the ground almonds and almond essence.

2. Lay two slices of bread, buttered-side down, on to the preheated plates and spoon over the fruit mixture. Cover with the remaining bread, buttered-side up.

3. Lower the lid and toast for about 2 minutes or until the bread is golden brown.

4. Serve warm with whipped cream.

NOTE

Adjust the almond flavouring to taste.

APPLE SCONES

Makes 3

450 g/1 lb cooking (tart) apples, peeled, cored and sliced
30 ml/2 tbsp water
15 ml/1 tbsp butter
50 g/2 oz sugar
2.5 ml/½ tsp cinnamon
A good squeeze of lemon juice
1 quantity Basic Fruit Scone Dough (see page 90)
Melted butter for brushing
To serve:
Fresh cream

1. Mix together all the ingredients in a pan except the dough and butter for brushing. Cover and simmer slowly until the apples are tender.

2. Remove the lid and continue to cook the apples, mashing them with a wooden spoon as they simmer, until the apple is a thick purée. Put to one side to cool.

3. Roll out the scone dough and cut six 13 cm/5 in squares. Brush one side of each square with melted butter and lay two, buttered-side down, on to the preheated plates.

4. Spoon over some of the apple purée and cover with squares of dough, buttered-side up.

5. Lower the lid, but do not clip the handles together, and cook for 4 minutes or until the dough is golden.

6. Repeat with the remaining ingredients and serve with fresh cream.

CHOCOLATE AND APRICOT MUNCHIES

Serves 2

4 chocolate digestive biscuits (Graham crackers), crushed

200 g/7 oz canned apricots, well-drained and chopped

15 ml/1 tbsp apricot jam (conserve)

4 slices of bread, buttered on one side with Caramel Butter
(see page 94)

To serve:

Custard or whipped cream

1. Mix the biscuits, apricot and jam in a bowl.

2. Lay two slices of bread, buttered-side down, on to the
   preheated plates and spoon over the biscuit mixture.
   Cover with the remaining slices of bread, buttered-
   side up.

3. Lower the lid and toast for about 2–3 minutes, or until
   the bread is golden brown.

4. Serve warm, with custard or whipped cream.

VARIATIONS
Use any crushed biscuits (cookies) and fruit of your choice.
Fresh fruit, peeled, cored and chopped, can be used instead
of canned.

TOASTING TIP
Sweet fillings, such as jam (conserve) or pie fillings retain
their heat longer than savoury fillings, so allow the toasties
to cool for a few minutes before eating. Pricking them with
a fork after toasting helps to cool them down. Sprinkling
5 ml/1 tsp of sugar on the outside before toasting makes
the lining crisper.

TREACLE TARTS

Makes 2

175 g/6 oz frozen shortcrust pastry, thawed
Melted butter, for brushing
Grated rind of ½ lemon
15 ml/1 tbsp lemon juice
60 ml/4 tbsp golden (light corn) syrup
50 g/2 oz cornflakes, crushed
To serve:
Custard

1. Roll out the pastry to approximately 25 cm/10 in square and cut into four smaller squares. Brush one side with melted butter.

2. Mix the grated lemon rind with the lemon juice, golden syrup and cornflakes to form a soft consistency.

3. Lay two slices of pastry, buttered-side down, on to the preheated plates and spoon over the cornflake mixture. Cover with the remaining slices of pastry, buttered-side up.

4. Lower the lid, without clipping the handles together, and cook for 4 minutes or until the pastry is golden brown.

5. Serve warm with custard or leave to cool before serving cold.

TUTTI-FRUTTI TREATS

Makes 3

---

100 g/4 oz coconut macaroons, crushed

---

10 glacé (candied) cherries, chopped

---

25 g/1 oz raisins

---

30 ml/2 tbsp clear honey

---

6 slices of raisin bread, buttered on one side

---

1. **Mix all the ingredients together, except the bread. Stir well.**

2. **Lay two slices of raisin bread, buttered-side down, on to the preheated plates and spoon over some of the fruit mixture. Cover with slices of raisin bread, buttered-side up.**

3. **Lower the lid and toast for about 2 minutes or until the bread is golden brown.**

4. **Repeat with the remaining ingredients and serve warm.**

VARIATION

Try using chocolate-coated macaroons, which give a lovely chocolate flavour to the treats.

TOASTING TIP

Delicious fruit pies can be made in your sandwich toaster. Use puff pastry squares with stewed fruit or canned fruit pie fillings to create instant desserts. Spread puff pastry with sweet mincemeat to make delicious mince pies at Christmas. Serve with brandy butter.

FRUIT AND NUT CRUNCHIES

Makes 3

50 g/2 oz rolled oats
50 g/2 oz shelled walnuts, chopped
50 g/2 oz dates, chopped
1 small eating (dessert) apple, peeled, cored and chopped
30 ml/2 tbsp apricot jam (conserve)
6 slices of bread, buttered on one side
To serve:
Custard or whipped cream

1. **Mix all the ingredients together, except the bread.**

2. **Lay two slices of bread, buttered-side down, on to the preheated plates and spoon over some of the fruit and nut mixture. Cover with slices of bread, buttered-side up.**

3. **Lower the lid and toast for about 2–3 minutes until the bread is golden brown.**

4. **Serve these delicious crunchies warm with custard or whipped cream.**

QUICK BAKEWELL TARTS

Makes 2

100 g/4 oz cake crumbs (e.g. Madeira)
30 ml/2 tbsp ground almonds
1.5–2.5 ml/¼–½ tsp almond essence (extract)
1 large egg yolk
175 g/6 oz frozen shortcrust pastry, thawed
Melted butter, for brushing
Raspberry or blackcurrant jam (conserve) for spreading
To serve:
Custard or whipped cream

1. Mix the cake crumbs, almonds and essence in a bowl and add the egg yolk to form a stiff mixture.

2. Roll out the pastry to approximately 25 cm/10 in square and cut into four smaller squares.

3. Brush one side with melted butter and the other side with jam. Lay two squares of pastry, buttered-side down, on to the preheated plates. Quickly spoon over the cake mixture and cover with the remaining slices of pastry, buttered-side up.

4. Lower the lid, but do not clip the handles together, and cook for about 3–4 minutes, or until the pastry is golden brown.

5. Serve warm with custard or cold with whipped cream.

CURRANT CAKES
Makes 3

10 ml/2 tsp butter
10 ml/2 tsp soft brown sugar
100 g/4 oz currants
50 g/2 oz candied peel, chopped
2.5 ml/½ tsp mixed (apple-pie) spice
225 g/8 oz frozen puff pastry, thawed
Butter, for brushing
Sugar, for sprinkling
To serve:
Custard

1. Melt the butter in a pan and stir in the brown sugar, currants, candied peel and spice. Mix well and leave to cool.

2. Roll out the pastry and cut out six 13 cm/5 in squares. Brush lightly with butter on one side.

3. Lay two squares, buttered-side down, on to the preheated plates and quickly spoon over some of the currant mixture. Cover with squares of pastry, buttered-side up.

4. Lower the lid, but do not clip the handles together, and cook for about 3 minutes or until the pastry is golden brown and crisp.

5. Repeat with the remaining ingredients.

6. Sprinkle with sugar while still hot. These are delicious served with custard.

PASTRIES AND DOUGHS

As I have mentioned before, shortcrust and puff pastry, as well as dough, can be cooked surprisingly well in a sandwich toaster. For convenience, I would recommend you use packet mixes for dough and either chilled or frozen shop-bought shortcrust and puff pastry. (If using frozen, make sure you thaw it first.)

When using pastry, roll it out thinly and cut it slightly larger than the plates on your toaster as it tends to shrink. Cut it into approximately 13 cm/5 in squares. Brush one side of each square with melted butter, oil or margarine and place them, buttered-side down on to the bottom plates. Add your chosen filling and cover with the top piece, buttered-side up. Lower the lid, but do not clip the handles together, and cook for about 3–4 minutes, or until the pastry is crisp and brown. Trim off any excess pastry after cooking. The quantities stated for pastry in the recipes refer to ready-made weight.

BASIC CHOUX PASTRY

Makes approximately 10 choux buns

15 ml/1 tbsp butter
120 ml/4 fl oz water
50 g/2 oz plain (all-purpose) flour
A pinch of salt
2 large eggs, beaten

1. Place the butter and water in a saucepan and bring to the boil.

2. Remove the pan from the heat and immediately add the flour and salt all at once. Beat the mixture until the dough comes away from the side of the pan.

3. Gradually beat in the eggs until the mixture is smooth, thick and glossy.

4. Place heaped 15 ml/1 tbsp of the mixture on the oiled, preheated plates and use as directed in the recipes.

NOTE

If your model has sectioned plates, place 15 ml/1 tbsp in each section on both sides of the cutter. For appliances that have dished plates, drop 15 ml/1 tbsp on each plate. Lower the lid but do not clip the handles together, and cook for about 8-10 minutes until the buns are golden brown and crisp. Remove from the toaster and split open one side of each bun to allow the steam to escape and to prevent them from becoming soggy. Leave to cool on a wire rack.

COOKING TIP

The pastry will rise during cooking and may push the lid of the sandwich toaster open. Do not be tempted to force the lid down as the pastry will not become light and crisp.

BASIC YEAST DOUGH

Makes approximately 4–5 pizzas

10 ml/2 tsp dried yeast
5 ml/1 tsp sugar
350 ml/12 fl oz luke-warm water
450 g/1 lb plain (all-purpose) flour
5 ml/1 tsp salt

1. Mix together the dried yeast and sugar and sprinkle over the luke-warm water. Leave to stand for about 15–20 minutes until the mixture is frothy.

2. Sift the flour and salt into a large bowl. Make a well in the centre and pour in the yeast mixture.

3. Mix to a stiff dough. Turn the dough on to a lightly floured board and knead for about 8 minutes until it is smooth and elastic.

4. Place in an oiled polythene bag and leave in a warm place to rise for about 45 minutes or until the dough has doubled in size.

5. Punch the dough down, knead lightly and roll out very thinly. Use as required in recipes.

NOTE

The dough needs to be made about an hour before you need it, as it has to rise in a warm place.

BASIC SCONE DOUGH

Makes approximately 2–3 pizzas

175 g/6 oz self-raising (self-rising) flour
2.5 ml/½ tsp baking powder
15 ml/1 tbsp margarine
90 ml/6 tbsp milk

1. Mix together the flour and baking powder.

2. Rub in the margarine and mix with the milk to form a firm, soft dough.

3. Roll out fairly thinly and cut into approximately 13 cm/ 5 in squares and use as required in recipes.

BASIC FRUIT SCONE DOUGH

Follow the recipe and method for Basic Scone Dough. Stir 25 g/1 oz sugar and 25 g/1 oz sultanas (golden raisins) into the mixture before adding the milk. Use as required in recipes.

NOTE

This basic scone dough can be used as an alternative lining for pizzas. Simply double the quantity if you wish to make a large number of pizzas.

FLAVOURED BUTTERS

FEED ME

The addition of savoury or sweet flavourings to butter or margarine will make your toasties or rolls more interesting. They will prove a delicious change from plain butter or margarine when spread on all kinds of breads and linings. Covered well, the butters will keep in the refrigerator for up to two weeks. Butter for sandwiches should be soft enough to spread easily and is better removed from the refrigerator approximately an hour before using. For each recipe, simply combine the ingredients together and use as required (ingredients may be adjusted to suit individual preferences).

ANCHOVY BUTTER

Use with fish, chicken or meat fillings.

100 g/4 oz butter, softened
15–30 ml/1–2 tbsp anchovy paste
5 ml/1 tsp lemon juice
Black pepper

CURRY BUTTER

Use with egg, lamb, chicken or vegetable fillings.

100 g/4 oz butter, softened
5–10 ml/1–2 tsp curry powder
5 ml/1 tsp lemon juice

HERB BUTTER

Use with any savoury filling.

100 g/4 oz butter, softened
10 ml/2 tsp mixed dried herbs
5 ml/1 tsp lemon juice
Salt and pepper

GARLIC BUTTER

Use with any savoury filling.

100 g/4 oz butter, softened
2 garlic cloves, crushed
A squeeze of lemon juice
Salt and pepper

LEMON BUTTER
Use with fish or chicken fillings.

100 g/4 oz butter, softened

10 ml/2 tsp lemon rind, finely grated

5 ml/1 tsp lemon juice

2–3 drops Tabasco or hot pepper sauce

MUSTARD BUTTER
Use with meat, cheese or fish fillings.

100 g/4 oz butter, softened

10 ml/2 tsp prepared English mustard

TOMATO BUTTER
Use with lamb, bacon, ham, cheese or shellfish fillings.

100 g/4 oz butter, softened

15 ml/1 tbsp tomato purée (paste)

A good pinch of nutmeg

2.5 ml/$\frac{1}{2}$ tsp lemon juice

Salt and pepper

SWEET LEMON OR ORANGE BUTTER

Use with any sweet filling.

100 g/4 oz unsalted (sweet) butter, softened

5–10 ml/1–2 tsp lemon or orange rind

5 ml/1 tsp lemon or orange juice

15 ml/1 tbsp icing (confectioners') sugar, sifted

CARAMEL BUTTER

Use with any sweet filling.

100 g/4 oz butter, softened

50 g/2 oz soft brown sugar

CINNAMON BUTTER

Use with any sweet filling.

100 g/4 oz butter, softened

2.5 ml/½ tsp ground cinnamon

INDEX

FEED ME

INDEX